# LUNAR DRIFT

# LUNAR DRIFT

## Marlene Cookshaw

Brick Books

Library and Archives Canada Cataloguing in Publication

Cookshaw, Marlene
        Lunar drift / Marlene Cookshaw.

Poems.
ISBN 1-894078-46-2

I. Title.

PS8555.O573L84 2005      C811'.54      C2005-903459-9

We acknowledge the Canada Council for the Arts, the
Government of Canada through the Book Publishing Industry
Development Program (BPIDP), and the Ontario Arts Council
for their support of our publishing program.

Cover art: Original image from www.photos.com.

The author's photograph is by Mitchell Parry.

The book is set in Sabon and Rotis.

Design and layout by Alan Siu.

Printed by Sunville Printco Inc.

Brick Books
431 Boler Road, Box 20081
London, Ontario  N6K 4G6
www.brickbooks.ca

30 Years Young
Brick Books 1975–2005

*In reality we are always between two times: that of the body and that of consciousness... The soul is first, and above all, the locus of another time.*

— John Berger,
  *And Our Faces, My Heart,*
  *Brief as Photos*


*the dream of order draws us as surely
as the dream of freedom*

— Moya Cannon,
  "Murdering the Language"

# Contents

## Time's Arrow

## in illo tempore

# Time's Arrow

*... the truth was*
*time was moving in one direction, like a wave lifting*
*the whole house, the whole village*

—Louise Glück, "Radium"

## Dial

Long before we had time in hand,
this much was clear: possession is never

fulfillment of want. Want trumpets
its own declaration. Before breath is drawn

the lungs erect their own cathedraled ribs.
Double-edged and variable, want

so awes us that the thing desired
stands in for it, the way a whiff of latakia

lifts you, old man, in its arms,
or a tune not heard for years revives

the voice that was a wife.
The clock repeats that error

in each numbered slice. Its face
encapsulates a want so huge

it blinds us to ourselves. We need
to own what's missed: we have forgotten

that the index is our keen revolving earth.
We think the numbers signifying stars

eclipse its scale. They don't. Earth
is the spinning heart that leans

in their direction. Over time we transfer
more than our allegiance. Meanwhile,

the invention of zero. Meanwhile the ozone
unbuttons its coat.

## Nilometer

Early, the most accurate looked down,
not up. Farmers lined the Nile's mud with reeds
and notched them, watched

the river rise. And to the day it rose, to Thoth's day,
offering the seasons, nearly equal,
of flood and growth and harvest. Floodwaters

cued the New Year. The people called it *sea*.
Second-longest river on the earth,
a calendar four thousand miles long and

tangible. The first known date in human history
comes down to us: 4241 B.C. Twelve months
of thirty days, and five birthdays of the gods:

Osiris, Isis, Horus, Nephthys, Set. Then
someone human looked back at the sky,
admitted Sirius, the Dog Star, bright companion

of the rising sun at flood. It told the people
they were out a quarter-day. Two thousand years
would pass till Caesar knew. Still nothing changed.

The priests, devoted to the river, would not have it.
They set their truth on the Nile's tongue, which
lapped the desert's teeth and soaked the reed.

## Lunar Drift

The blessing of the phrase, its grace.
First deer skirting the edge of the birch grove
at dusk when you've ceded the hunt.
Breeze like a breath. Hand of the beloved
after a long drought. Hush now, it
wheels the sky's brow and closes our eyes.
Moonlight upon us, we're lulled.
Inhale, exhale, die awhile, return.
After the time of sprout-kale and
the month of storms will soon come
Eostur-monath. Then, Thromilchi—joy month—
when milk cows seek our hands three times a day.
But numbers are the problem. How many
months? Twelve of those twenty-nine-and-a-half-day breaths
are not enough, thirteen too many. Soon
Winterfylleth no longer marks the start of winter,
in Scere-monath the sheep are sheared too early,
and hungry wolves come to the village
when Wulf-monath is past. The moon,
its pull, is only half the story. Hold
its geared perfection in your head and,
next to it, the sun's slide through the seasons.
Their teeth don't meet. The equinox comes at us
every spring. Sun rules our work. We call that fixed.
The moon is in our blood: we say it drifts.

## Armillary

I only came to watch. I hate when actors
breach the fourth wall. Though any wall's
a moot point out of doors.
I've always been the sort that
wants a second run at life,
the first time through to scout things out,
then, mindful, make another pass.
This performance promises to take us all.
The artist moves us through the park, one
at a time, according to the script.
He rides me on the crossbar of his bike.
The script dictates the bar must run
the length of my left thigh; it says what music
drives his pedalled strokes. He drops me
uphill from the others, in an open
grove amid spring lawn, daisies—small ones—
in the grass, and those miniscule
blue trumpets that make you think
you're seeing stars.

I take position on the ball of my left foot
and push off with the right. Rooted,
branches spread. After a bit, propulsion's
not required: I'm on a slope,
my leafy weight on the downward arc
enough to seal the orbit.
                              Eureka! Arrival
at the place where what's about to happen
finds you. I don't think what the others do, or
where. The artist has settled us all on our points
and will, at the right time, collect us. Part
of something and entirely myself, I spin
like a planet, a moon, anchored, vibrant
among birches, on the lee of a green slope,
river and city in sight. It's what
I was made for. Nobody watches,
or they do and it doesn't matter. I drive
the auger of my body, which drives
this green earth.

# Intercalation

Spiking the already-is.
The arrogance of that,
the gut-disturbed delight.

The Roman priests reserved
the right. Here is a day that
wasn't; here are eighty.

To stick one's nose in where
no thing is wanted. To want,
and thereby sidle up

to Schrödinger's cat, to watch
the stars wink out, and count them.
We dance or we look at our feet.

Each life's a vein of sediment
between before and after. We can
apologize for this, eat our dinner

in the dining hall's off-hours.
We can delude ourselves awhile:
the game won't stop. Take, eat.

The earth's our body. The Colca
Canyon on Peru's Pacific coast
is a surgery through sixteen thousand feet

of granite. What it reveals, between
the frigid Humboldt current and the ice cliffs
of the Andes, is everyday. Are these

prawns or tortellini? Trilobites?
What, ossified,
can we line our pockets with

to insulate ourselves against
tomorrow's loss?

## Ptolemy uses a quadrant to gauge the altitude of the moon

*The stars were foolish, they were not worth waiting for.*
*The moon was shrouded, fragmentary.*
*Twilight like silt covered the hills.*
*The great drama of human life was nowhere evident—*
—Louise Glück, "Screened Porch"


A swallow plummeted onto the basement sill.
A snake lifted its head to the mower. When
my husband phoned I was a thousand miles and a year
away from our shared home, and what I grieved
was less their deaths than the capacity to bear
the lives we're given. We deplore
the downed, the broken; imagining
an interrupted arc to the ideal. More real
were disappointments we took, cloudy evenings, to the shore.
*The stars were foolish, they were not worth waiting for.*

At dawn, the churr of the woodpecker, ravenous
bird. Our hearts were human and not
up to its insistence. Only two fears we had,
a countable number, between us, what
you might expect: on the one hand, we were islanded,
embodied, and in time required to bury
a beloved dog, the ducks within our care, a young doe
stopped one night beneath the poplars—weary, we thought,
then paced out a grave. No wonder we grew wary.
*The moon was shrouded, fragmentary*

in the night sky, where, on the other hand,
the words we spoke distilled to meaningless
pricks of light. We feared our bodies, our minds
laboured, and in response, hypothesized
a third position, measured our displacement.
What we dreamed became a test of wills.
Love was not lacking, but it paled in light of how
hope rose repeatedly to the whirling
blade. Or, bloodily astonished, tumbled to the sills.
*Twilight like silt covered the hills,*

substantially higher than two millennia ago when
Ptolemy climbed with his brass instrument, awaiting dark.
What can he have been thinking? That earth was shiftless
underfoot, stable beneath the ladder his mind was making
up? And why? What good to calibrate the distance
between who we are and what we might lament
becoming? There will be always there; here,
here. To know by how much we fall short?
He set his jaw, released the arrow of his gaze, intent:
*The great drama of human life was nowhere evident—*

## 46 B.C.

In the Year of Confusion were four hundred
forty-five days. In a bath in the middle
of the afternoon I pour ginger-lily oil and musk.

The floor lamp's dimmed till all I can read is
our past in shards, dug up, partial as crockery
in the garden. In the Year of Confusion

were four hundred forty-five days. I dream
I've set an armful of linens at the garden gate,
and wander between the beds, uprooting

Queen Anne's lace. There is time for this.
I look up to see my old dog curled tight
in the heap of quilts. Joy is that carrot scent

unearthed. What pierces, awake, is his absence,
eight years dead. In the Year of Confusion
were four hundred forty-five days. I lie down

to Keith Jarrett's piano. He is gone in the sound.
One chord after the other. Lost. Found. That dark
interval. Each surge repeated, changed.

To think like that. Open-mouthed. Let me
wail, or say anything wholly; let me not whimper.

## Water-Driven Spherical Bird's-Eye-View Map of the Heavens

First the clepsydra, the 'stolen water'
by which speech was measured

in a Roman court of law. Simple:
the tiny orifice, scaled reservoir

from which or into which the water
dripped. Its use for centuries widespread,

though Julius Caesar ground his teeth
at how, in British campaign winters,

the freezing of the waterclocks
threw his night watches into disarray.

I-Xing was first to automate, in 725 A.D.,
a bronze and iron structure cased in wood.
The water-driven wonder tracked the stars
and planets in their drift. It followed time,
and only incidentally kept it.

Charlemagne, that great collector, received one
as a gift. From Baghdad: The Great Waterclock
of Sultan Harun al-Rashid, Fifth Caliph
of the Abbasid, Master of the Islamic World,
and, to all readers since, the sultan of *1001 Nights*.

Charlemagne liked gifts; he delighted
in the tilt of each bright ball nudged
by the waterwheel to ring a cymbal underneath,
in the twelve horsemen who stepped out
to end each hour and close the previous door.

This marvel charmed him more than the silk
robes, perfumes, ointments, that came with it,
more than the Persian tent, beside whose scented
opulence, having tramped the several thousand miles,
was staked the baffled, solitary elephant.

*The heavens move without ceasing, but so also
does water flow,* said Su Sung to those who gaped

in 1092 at his four-year accomplishment: elegant
instrument which synthesized all schools.

Three dozen scoops caught water on a wheel
twice human height that drove the shafts and chains

of the construction, its pagoda doors and manikins
and bells and drums. Thirty feet above the ground

it peaked in a bronze armillary sphere, the celestial
imagined rings cast bronze and borne by dragons.

(And still the water froze, despite the torches.)

## Stand In

Like the ominous cuckoo of the pagan wood, which
though it sang two notes—the light, the dark—
yet by its actions orchestrated
the fleeting lives of wrens and pipits,

the jacquemart of the public clock
arrived to order ours. Entowered, armed, he
signalled interruption of the flow of time
and oversaw the use of it.

The Crusaders made of him a captured Moor,
and this animated figure, hostage to the iron
weight's compulsion, supplanted our sentient
to and fro. We abandoned place.

The jacquemart was a double of the man
formerly employed to strike the chimes, who,
celebrated in his village, rang the changes,
invented melodies to greet the hours.

Then industry struck a deal with metal
and forged a mechanism strong enough
to ring the tower bells unaided. And so
the jacquemart, representing human interest,

re-membered us, our sounding of the gateway
in the analemmic loop—that twisted orbit—between
the guiding palm of the sun's arc and
the seductive compensation of the moon's.

We gave up attending to the pulse of time,
turnstiled it, focused on our labour. We left
unnoted the disturbance of the spirits of the air.
We left time to its own devices.

# The Great Astronomical Clock of Strasbourg

One of seven, one of the numbered
wonders. Erected while a third of Europe
succumbed to the Black Death, its iron
axle, pulley, weights affirmed God's

regulation of a clockwork world.
Pinnacled and pillared, tiled, ornate
in 1352, but of insufficient magic
to astronomers two centuries advanced.

In 1574, they rebuilt it to embody
everything they knew: revolutions
of the planets, phases of the moon,
eclipse, equations for conversion

of the sun and moon to local time.
Times: sidereal, apparent. Chariots
wheel in and out of cloud, bearing
in turn the seven pagan gods. Today

it's Jupiter. And also, by the inner dial,
St Andrew. See, he bears his cross.
By the perpetual calendar we may discern
precession of the equinoxes, when

to marry, also the movable feasts, which
we may celebrate at lunch with friends,
at dinner with our ancestors in paradise.
Dominicals foretell red letter days.

Should it prove difficult to find yourself in this,
just listen: every quarter-hour will locate
you, struck in turn by Infancy, then
Adolescence, Manhood, and Old Age.

Time as number is almost incidental.
It's morning. At noon the twelve apostles
will swing by, be blessed by Christ.
An iron cock will flap and crow.

## A Precise Chronology

To the pressing query of the century—
when time began—his was not the first response.
Nor did he give his answer lightly. James Ussher
travelled, mused; he bought or copied
a priceless library of early script; he watched the sky.

He ventured each step carefully, factoring in
all that anyone could think of: clues
the Holy Ghost had planted, historical accounts,
star charts, the slippage of the calendar against
the seasons, the number of begats. Also

destruction of his property, estrangement
from his homeland, gravity, the Troubles.
He gave the best sum of a reasonable life.
Creation, he said, *fell upon the entrance of the night
preceding the twenty-third day of October* in 4004 B.C.,

this a Sunday *nearest the Autumnal Aequinox,
notwithstanding the stay of the sun
in the dayes of Joshua, and the going back of it*
for Ezekiah. This verdict offered up in Latin
in 1650: *The Annals of the World*, and four years later

his wife Phoebe died. All of his singular life brought
to a question absurdly reduced. Who are we to ridicule,
or even doubt the tally? We who, ruined by news, take
everything on hearsay. He lived three-quarters of a century.
After the Troubles destroyed his land he never went home.

He gave the best sum of a laboured contemplation
and was respected in his life. The King James Bible
endorsed his *first motion of time,* and Isaac Newton
clung to it against all findings. Cromwell insisted on
Westminster Abbey when he died.

Archbishop of Armagh and Primate of All Ireland,
Vice-Chancellor of Trinity College,
St Patrick the apostle's hundredth heir.
His grave was marked in 1904 by Irish
marble, with Latin lettering in brass.

Born of Arland and Margaret, brother to Ambrose,
he married Phoebe, his wife of forty years,
fathered Elizabeth, in time became *most learned
among the holy, most holy among the learned*
and in 1656 he *fell asleep in Christ.*

# Reckoning

*To feel yourself wake into change, as if your change*
*Were immense and figured into the heavens' longing.*
                    —Mark Strand, *Dark Harbor,* "VII"

As in sea voyages before clocks were trusted,
we're given latitudes to navigate. Pirates, currents

haunt each favoured route. A girl, a ship
may face an ambush in those narrows. What

to do? She drifts. Then meaning
freights the fact that she dreams every night of

boats. *The moon a ghostly.* Writing is embarking,
buoyant, on the unknown, with maybe the mere

glimmer of where she wants to go—which is
not always, even often, where anyone arrives.

Longitude escapes us. She sails
by dead reckoning, estimating track

and distance from her last uncertainty. Dashed
against rocks, foreign coasts or the unachievable

horizon, all hands lost, she washes up
bloated on beaches. And ships herself again.

For the waves' ride, the water's sheer
intelligence, for how it veers and seethes and doubles

back. But the beach? The shore? What earthly reason?
Liquid, the condition anticipating nothing, unfolds

a soft accordion—time's corrugated din—
tumbling its limber mass, skin over skin.

# Pocketwatch

*Thought constructs itself in the world of material objects....*
*Consciousness itself was made possible, linguists suggest, only when*
*language constructed a metaphorical "space" in which it could live.*
—Jane Hirshfield, "The Question of Originality"

Hatchling of the Nuremberg egg,
the pocketwatch pecks free from etymology:
it wakes no one, for naught, and sleeps
in a vest pocket, though the odd one plays a tune
or winds its mechanism by the strides and gestures
of the man who flaunts it. In this way
it distinguishes, each from the other: encased
in horn or sharkskin or enamelled with a minuet
or inlaid with the family crest in shell.

From weight to coiled spring: in one transition
we're disconnected from the common
calling to assembly, mass, or work. We beg to differ
about which of us approaches the true
solar noon. Freed from the village clock,
then from the mantel of the family, now
we have time in hand; we think we manage it.

Meanwhile, time, suspended, draws as near as
our own skin. We believe this means it is at our
disposal, a laughable error carried across
centuries. The further we withdraw from flux
the closer we clutch its measure, investing the intricate
works with sapphires, rubies, buying time, coining
privacy, inventing dislocation.

## Idiots Savants

Twins, mathematical wizards,
plump-thighed in plaid trousers,

Tweedledum, Tweedledee, they
delighted in singing the numbers they saw.

Vaudeville, mama's boys, a whole
century between them, tapped into

a field that answers all questions
before they've been posed. They don't know

what they do. They just see the numbers.
No computation, deduction, projection, follow-

through, clean up after yourselves.
No *lights out, time to get up, wash dishes,*

*feed dogs.* This is the big time: numbers
twenty-four digits long and irreducible. No

*no climbing trees, no reading in bed,*
*no dessert before meals.* Piece of cake.

*No touching the furnace, the ornaments, china,*
*the telephone, keys.* Instead: cardinals, fractions.

*Don't fidget in church, don't talk while*
*I'm talking.* Meaningless

numbers they sing, a means. Notes
to call back a new chorus:

Awe. Incredulity. Breathless delight.

# Residual

*If travel is searching*
*and home has been found...*
—Björk, "Hunter"

I believe there are details of the eagle bone I need
to know; I believe I cannot write the poem until
I know them. These details mill about in the gully

over the next rise, pawing the early snow for moss.
In summer they raise 13,000-year-old dust.
Only a week ago I watched the white skirts

of a plunging eagle as it skid talons-first
down to the bay. Saw the mallard pinwheel,
panicked, for the overhang of shore.

But what we're talking of is bone.
What doesn't burn up, what reduces
last, and so incorporates the soul.

Eagle bone would be the soul of hunting,
bright bird-eye salted, muscle reabsorbed.
The mineral of time made portable, made

tool. All the feathered nonsense strewn.
What draws disperses. That's the rule.
The hunter at the cave mouth tests his edge.

What he can't see but knows will pass
desires him. Each time,
the narrow moon after a heavy frost,

the herd is on the far side of a thickened air.
His expectation slows the hunt. He holds
the eagle bone. He wants what bridges.

For days he's camped, alone, sufficient,
but partial in his longing, like
the snow that falls now without wind.

He tries to cut a reindeer from the murk, to fix
through the blur of their repeated passage
the clearing where they graze. To do this

he softens muscle, breath; he slows
his blood. Exhaling, he opens
senses one by one, sight last. He aims

to bring the animal into being, bring
its being into antler, sinew, stink.
He must be here and not here: trick

with time, outline
the beast in its liminal migration.
If he holds his own, he gets what's needed

from the laggards, from the crippled,
or the angular unruly young. That turn
of the head that names him, that current

of regard, a round-eyed *ah*. The speech,
the courage, in their gaze.
If he doesn't hold his own, it fails.

Then where is joy? The animal
not here. Bone hollow.
In the sky a moon dispassionate

as eagle claw. What can we bear
to look at? If experience
is fractured, what to count on?

## *in illo tempore*

Imagine: a trail made of moments rather than minutes, wild bits of time which resist elapsing according to a schedule.

—Don McKay, "Baler Twine"

## Blue-Eyed Grass

Sitting on a bench that slopes to the pond,
waiting for fish to rise. The brush ticks.

The first marsh marigolds button a fall of
stones under the blue pump. The sun

comes out and goes in again. Southwest,
a grouse thumps a hesitant drum,

guinea fowl ratchet the east. Now fish
are rising, half-hearted, smallest first.

What are those tiny blue-faced flowers
in the grass? All that we are.

Later, red leaves, bronze, under
the plum tree's froth: peony shoots.

And maybe a finger of trillium. Maybe
a voice of god in this light. An engine

shudders the ribcage so briefly
all but its passing escapes us.

## List

Hammocked between sleep and
wakefulness, remarking dreams
as they dissolved, I got up to the start of
what I knew. Began to
list.
    What I'd heard on the roof
had sounded so like a familiar
rain. And yet. Trees
threshed the air.
          I took disillusion
like a flight of stairs
to the window nook. We need
to act, by which redream the past,
until we've learned
          a frequency, a gesture,
to answer all it asks. We either know
this dreaming to be what our lives embody
or we don't. It goes on all the same,

until our souls, exhausted,
haul themselves up from
sleep, through that blue syrup of commotion
in which we're neither there nor
here.
    Repeated, sound locates us.

Daylight, work, ignore the sonorous:
the planet's tremor, the carillon
of stars. We need the dark. It's only fear
out there; I know this.
          The queer ripple
in my shoulder blades, below my nape,
is product of the same position held

too long, bent over books and paper, reducing
all that passes
          to its intersection

with a pitch, transcribed.
                            Although
there's truth in this, it's not
the only. What of dreams, for
instance? Dance? As when

this morning a healer slipped her hand
beneath my skull, put thumb and finger
to my chin. In time
                          my head began to waft,
a poppy on its stem. The wonder of it was

I could not tell if hands or head
moved first, so fluid was the undulation,
freed of gravity, attuned
to something tidal. Breath. We
either know this dreaming or we don't.

Daylight, work: the wonder
goes on all the same.

## Redbreast

In the old farmhouse, dawn,
in April when the trees were bare

of everything but bloom, I woke
alone. And after dozing—now it's June—

I wake again in a cabin among mountains
to the queer shimmer of a gathering

storm, throw back my blanket, rise
to swing ajar the heavy door. Listen, the sky's

about to roar. The evergreens exhale
the redolent, dusty, too-warm smell that's

chaos: earth and air and water, mixed.
Before I found the lump in my left breast

my body dreamed a light
hard to ignore, blue-white, then hot

as fear. And hard:
small egg that slithered

on a ridge of bone. Would not
be gone, no matter, having wakened,

that my fingers tried to iron flat
the horror, almost hourly.

Three weeks' wait to learn its name.
I continued hanging laundry, loved

while holding something back, woke
and slept and dreamed of my dead parents,

my mother plump again—her speckled
housedress, lotioned arms!—my father

washing plates, his sleeves rolled up,
and talking: rain, old calendars, and seed.

Sound seen, transmuted, ultra.
Nothing I heard, nothing, lying

on my side, odalisque in boots
and denim, naked to the waist. The idea

this: that sound—
a woman shimmying the steel mouth of it

between her palm and my breast
and looking elsewhere—would free me

of all fear. It didn't. If not now, when?
And if not me, then why so many?

The screen was planetary: Saturn
in a sea of rings. Black

hole. Eclipse. Nothing
but a globe of fluid the sound waves

hurtled through. Perfectly
harmless.

To celebrate, my love and I
bought whiskey, Irish, a brand we hadn't

seen before—Redbreast, its pear-shape
cradled from the truck to the apartment door,

along a corridor of lawn pinned by a single tree
we'd passed a hundred times. In it

a nest I can't imagine having missed: perfect
bowl, half-coconut, upon whose rim a robin,

curved breast saturated red, kept watch
with her uncanny kohl-rimmed eye.

Within a week I'd flown that earthly magic.
Into the mountains, to think, and worry up

some words. The day I left, the robin
showed what she was working on: two

squalling, wobble-jointed young.
The feeding, warming, guarding of them—

tyranny of infant need, of spring's
hot forwardness—employs her.

With every trip she makes away and back,
I'm lightened. Having bestowed on me

an otherworldly gift—this
problematic egg, its perfect

flicker, mild ache that pulls
my right hand to it like a child's drawing

of the nest, the tree—
the robin incubates. I speculate

on how to love this lump, to see it
new. Ecstatically, it dawns on me.

It must be painted blue.

## Brava

And if I give up, what
then? Give up, I mean,

the shell of who
I think myself to be. The still

life.
      Ah, little one, wanting
to negotiate a scenic route, the right

to drive, wanting to know
what to pack:
                  Nothing.

The barest sliver of yearning
goes forward, remakes you.

Nothing to do but look lovingly
at the upturned self,

kiss that uncomprehending
face goodbye.

## The Road Above the Falls

A might-be, partial trail, its goal uncertain,
challenges the cliff edge. I keep
to the road, and speculate why what contents me
is the known, the level, preconceived.

I stop to reconsider on a bench
so high my feet are airborne, swing
the other side of knees grown plump,
the right especially, whose numb flesh

thickened when a falling gravestone
made me reexamine the belief that
any of us had a leg to stand on. Yes,
it's true. Could I have made that up?

In any situation, what's paramount is
flux. Since I could swing my right foot
past my left and notice what went
on without my interference, ever since

I could object, take in the backhand
sting of just-a-minute, mind-your-business,
I've been bridging with my gaze, because
what's offered is irrational: a current

grappling with itself, a scrap of path
that mimics water's noise. I keep
my eye on both; I keep my distance.
The river and its shoreline then are family:

we navigate a route while jostling elbows,
keep what we can and watch our step.
I tell myself I'm staking
different turf, going my own way,

and that may be. Or maybe all we ever do
is strike a balance, bargain between
risks: desolate? diminished? Being
lost or being swallowed.

## What I Sprang From

Everyone gets the same deal, says the man on the radio.
From bitter cold I've stepped into this coffee shop, to thaw
the clenching of my back against the wind. The news

insists on skinny men with knives, lost hikers, cardiac arrest.
I'm on my way to town to find a history
of the fifties, what I sprang from, unprepared for weather.

Yesterday the woman massaging me left out
the middle of my body—no buttocks, breasts, internal organs—
making of me a starfish, all limbs and ligaments

too short on the left side. The waitress hums.
To get from here to town I must go out into the wind again—
same deal—mitts to my ears, lungs and legs cold-cramped.

The cars fly by, and gulls and crows head north, confusing
still points in the gusting clouds. A friend
has lent me this sweater, colour of river stones,

mussels we found on the rocks as kids: a smoky blue.
This friend and I watched *Three Faces of Eve*, and all night
I dreamed it ghosting my life with: *yes*

and *yes* and *yes*. Joanne Woodward as three
women in one slinky-skirted dress: beginning of the fifties,
Eve Black emerging from Eve White and, later, Jane,

who under protest kisses her dead grandmother,
remembers all her teachers, one by one. Then, of course,
both Eves will die, wink out—the doctor wins—and Jane alone

will raise hands to her face and speak:
Not here. There's nobody here but me.

# Fallow

I'm thinking how my life looks in the light of this
honey-paned lamp, pen in hand, smoke
curling over the roof peak. Years go up

in the rush of a passing car. My mother phones
to read the label from
her Persian Lilac after-bath refresher.

She's thanked me once for her birthday gift.
I figure she's maybe showered now and wants
to thank me all refreshed.

I'm standing downstairs at the kitchen phone,
gazing over the deck rail at the sodden
field between us and our neighbours in which

for years I've built a cottage in my head,
all picket-fenced and distant, in the lowest corner
my husband wants just left alone.

She asks what is the use
of the thing that's coloured, cardboard, sown
with flowers. The words won't stick. *Oh, that,*

I say, *that's not part of the gift; it's the package.*
Always these crossed wires, she and I,
inside and out, bewildered, how

to use what's there, and then
her voice trails off and disappears. She
doesn't answer my *hello*s, my *mom*s; the phone just stops

its mediation. I can't call anyone to check on her.
My line won't disconnect from our unfinished
argument. I pull on boots, prepare to cross the field.

## The Hour

On May's long grass
between the driveway ruts, our dog
lies on his back

and trembles, offers up
his infant old-man face

from which his ears
depend like tired wings:

he wills us not to leave.

And when we've left, he loops
those nearly endless limbs
in the forbidden leather chair,

to knot the hour, to brace
it like a stone against the river's quick

resolve, till we're washed home
again and tell him who he is.

## Another Rhapsody

Each afternoon at five, when evergreens
drain the sky's watery light, a train whistle

freights it, keening, into the hills. Holds it. Hold it. You
call too. As mothers used to from the threshold,

dusk, one hand smoothing a housedress,
the other flinging the screen door wide.

A *twenty-winged cloud of yellow butterflies,*
we're blind to our own beauty and what is common

in us. Our flesh embodies loneliness
and is the means to bridge it. We

were never meant for this. This is
exactly what we're meant for. Shared

flashlight beam on the snowy path and laughter
in the dark. We are sculpted

from butter and longing. Few of us
glimpse our own deaths, let alone

certainty. My friend who grieves for her father
says, "I will never get over this,"

and the apprehension of that is a second grief.
We move too fast because to slow down is to know

ourselves a little, our one wing and its gristled hinge,
arrhythmic heart, the monkish heroism of our feet.

When frogs strike up in April on a cloudless night
you'd swear it's stars that chime from the chaotic muck.

What they mutter of is not the point. The point is talk.
Not information, no more than diagnosis

of a buckled septum stands in for oxygen, efficiently conveyed.
What good to know, for instance, the exact length

of the string of eggs I'm born with, how many still
queue up, how long precisely a half-life? Close

your eyes. They manufacture distance,
distinguish predator from prey. They muddy sense.

The point is a stream of syllables approximating
song, which does not measure time

but sounds it, puts it
in its fluid place.

## Starved

In the middle of a noisy party three of us
have gathered, holding long-stemmed glasses up
between the pretzels and the door. One leans in
to ask if either of the others have seen death.

Her eyes are gleaming. Behind me someone
troubles someone else for smokes,
and a charming British traveller surveys
this nation's writers for their favourite names.

Well, why not? Inquire of death, I mean.
The tall young man begins an anecdote about a kind
of bird, a scavenger, that makes good
eating if you're starved—a whisky-jack, that's it—

while awestruck I'm brought up against,
in turn, my father's blue-lipped thud, my old dog
softening, like wax in sunlight, in my arms,
my mother's figurehead demeanour fixed

for days on that elusive port. Determined
though remorseful, he and his friend kill the bird,
and pluck and cook it. The traveller's list grows.
I believe at some point, having exhausted

narrative, the tall young man remembers
scattered drops of blood on snow.

## Hindsight

When I was eight a man leaned over me. He clicked
correction to my wide-eyed gaze, and I went home,
first saw the leaves on trees. First knew I saw them.

Since then those leaves have taken shape
and fallen forty times. I had thought
trees were other. Fogged haze above the ground.

And then discovered each leaf, backlit, gilded
as the hair beneath my father's Sunday sleeves,
as my own eyes, haloed by their rhinestone rims: alive.

What passes does not die but moves from focus. Love
is ocular, mundane. We are crosshairs, misaligned.

## Portrait of a Marriage

But I want to see, my husband says, holding
to his chest the fleshy dark-bound book, so I agree

to sit beside him on my mother's bed
with the album I've assembled of her past.

By that I mean the time before her birth, the rooms
she never saw but heard the stories of. They're posed

and sepia, of course, people I don't know
by name; I've framed their good materials

and lace and pinched expression, their absurdly
idle hands, with a broad mat. The tiny photos

are like mildly poison seeds in the black apple
that my husband hands me, bitter

ones that waste you over time. Although
the relatives are mine, no sooner have we sat,

the first page open on our laps, than, astonished,
my glance rises to a foreign prospect, framed.

Above the trinket-littered sill, beyond the breezy
yellow sheers, where square flat lawn should be,

then wide suburban avenue with periodic
cones of light, instead: a cityscape I've never seen.

Vanished, the barberry that ripped our arms when,
children, we were sent into its purple thorns

to turn the faucet on. The house transported. One
of a hillside of sooty frontages the colour

of dried blood. Joyless houses, homes of the hard-
working, cheek by jowl to nondescript. Iron

railings, narrow ledges, chimney pots, all
cramped beneath a lowering sky.

Inside's the same as always: my mother's
house, the room in which I watch her sleep,

a house grown small and cluttered with the years,
whose rooms I know like chambers of my heart.

I lay down the book and walk, uncertain,
from her room to mine; I slide the window up

and swivel out, bellying the brick the way I used to
as a child, lowering my bare feet to the dirt.

But this back yard's, like the front, transformed:
clearly exterior yet undisturbed by wind, a bluely

formal garden, furnished with vine-clambered
pergolas and trimmed box hedge. I pause

at the conversational aspiring of wisteria
and bittersweet, then look

beyond, below that to a winter orchard. Unfenced,
its border seems the atmosphere itself, cut

like a cube of glass. Seen from above,
in precise formation, dwarf trees

smock the tawny grass, each trunk a stitch
whose branches pucker the surrounding silk.

I cross the lawn. Stripped of bark
the silvery trees are hybrid of the wild

arbutus and those husbanded varieties of fruit
valued for their starry fizz upon the tongue.

Though winter, the polished limbs are opulent: globes
of frost and mica depend from branch tips,

crisp and glittering like icy jewels. Their beauty nourishes
the eye; indeed their luminosity's a substitute

for sun, here not acute enough to force
an aperture. I think their juices enter through the skin.

In the cluttered room between the back and front,
the thermostat is cranked to an invalid's decree.

Drugged by the heat and bleary in its amniotic
haze, my husband shuffles faces of the petulant, the smug

unhappy captured dead. He turns a page, then I, and,
vaguely hungry, we lean a little in each other's arms.

## Wiltshire Downs

Last fall the Old World wore a silver face:
the mime who bowed near courtyard violets

kissed my hand. He did this once and winked
and stalled. The sparrows fed between his boots.

*Behold, how good and pleasing,*
said the West Door of Bath Abbey. And it was,

even then, your mouth on mine. The drained pools
of the old city steamed sulphurous

and iron-rich as our new well
on land whose history we'd barely rubbed

the surface of. The Abbey's carapace
was caged and being

scrubbed. Mould, it seems, will eat away the stone,
and acid from the fingertips of those who

touch. You tell me now
what you've learned since: affairs are the enactment

of what isn't spoken. The mime who
moved so slowly kissed my hand. A year exactly

since the last time we made love. I know
the city, date, could find the bed.

There was no other for me then, except
the ghostly one you claimed I tried to make

you into. The Abbey walls were scaffolded and cleaned
halfway. The mime moved like a child's toy, wound up and

winding down. And stopping when? From this side
of the ocean, his skin's a mylar sheen

of pain. Impenetrable. Then, it dazzled. We knew him
by his white gloves, cane, and how he managed

to convince us there was no way out. We walked
the streets of Bath; we toured façades. What dreams

we built and how they held us up: the sweet
absurdity of the construction. Affairs

embodied what we could not speak.
We mimed it. Telling. A year later

there's no home, no marriage. What dissolves
is dream: the agony, our hand on that. Still

it does not matter that my heart's no longer housed;
it's larger, porous. The Abbey's central. From there

we travelled outward to the middens; we walked
stone circles; we eyed the White Chalk Horse.

## Savasana

My body mourns each body lost
since it awakened

to itself. Here, then
scattered; incorporate,

then gone. Is this memory
or colouring outside the lines?

The world would have me
string my life in one long

clotted chain suspending
each embrace. It's not like that.

I love at once: that arc's what
unifies, what sees me whole.

I would not undo any
of the knots that led me here, but

oh, I miss what's made and then
unmade me.

## Tuck Everlasting

In April the workmen disassemble the dead tree.

Upright but skeletal, it constellates
the view from our second-storey room, which opens
north through ornamental plum, horse chestnut,

into a row of trees I think are planes. One
split its bark last month and has been weeping sap.

Felled by the twin assaults of cramps and fever
I witness this from bed. My body's bled for weeks
in a bizarre forewarning it intends to stop.

The cherry-picker shudders, veers up
the windowpane, across. The fever raged
the first half of the night. Today the cramps

draw all my senses in; the outside world is glazed.
The man in yellow hardhat limb by limb reduces

its exploratory reach. A tree dying
in the country would feed woodpeckers, house ants, in time
succumb to gravity, capitulate, renew.

Here in the city, on the other hand:
annoyance, eyesore, vantage point for crows.
The dissevering of a single role is slow. In my lap

is a children's book, in which a magic spring
both dooms and blesses with eternal life.

Between the waves of pain I read, then stare
long moments north. The ornamental plum's

in leaf, bright copper dimpling
the glazing's lower half. Its blossoms
are both memory and promise. The casement

fronts the boulevard, horse chestnut greening
from the bottom up, and planes, one of which
unzipped its bark and spilled its insides out.

The workman reaches, lops and passes, drops
a segment from the bucket's other side. The silhouette
is sparer now, defined. He closes on what used to be

a growing tip—there were two always, really,
fallopial, and arcing greenly from the trunk.

## Porch

Though what I contemplate won't shift the rose's
thorned wrist from the threshold, or reanimate
the paper husks of bees, work is love is work.

Embroider that. Then look around. There is
only this bit of a life, what has silted up
in given corners. The front porch door ajar.

Do I really want a leafblower to get me out of this?
A broom has history: it stirs up if-I-hadn'ts, then
waits while the picket fence repaints itself. Curious,

insistent on a fair encounter, it allows
that any gesture's incomplete, sashays
the cheery lino with an aproned housedress

while the pushbroom's overgrown moustache
deals only with the beaten track, the shortest route
from here to there, and then it's only steps to the machine.

Here's to the inefficient: pause
for the cedar waxwings' rattle of the juniper,
berries hoisted for the journey south,

for the backflips of stubborn fluff and last year's
swallows' down and inhalation of the river's sludge.
Brooms encourage contemplation of the dust,

miserere for the unremovable. Meanwhile,
deaf and out of step, the neighbouring leafblower
fulminates a coughed-up dark and will not stop for air.

# Fox

Until last fall I'd never seen a fox, and then,
from a moving train, on a foreign track.

And, more than that, the fox was dead, tossed
to a ditch that trailed the outskirts of the city, end

of my marriage, though I didn't know that yet.
Its muzzle rested on its back. With the prescience

of the stricken, it had turned its head
to watch death overtake it. A year later, two days

before my forty-seventh birthday, another fox
trots past.      Fox! I think, and can't

sift out the meaning of its shape. Nothing flickers
with a red that true. And self-possessed: its walk

no more than twenty feet away so nonchalant
that all my programs threaten default, threaten

dance. Fox! Its unexpected breach of this world's
reasoned work. This far, no farther. Its

ordinary calm demeanour, keep-to-the-trail,
bomb-in-a-baby-carriage fur. Oh, farther, please.

Dear Ruth, I've seen a fox. Dear Mary-Rose, A riot
of such dignity just passed. I want more now,

the jay's note, eclipsing seasoned
thought, more than I know, more than

one man in my bed, whisky before noon,
the saxophone's bright veering

into trees. Yes, black-stockinged. Yes,
the tail: a streak of cedar, eucalyptus, sage.

And when the moon appears, it has a fox's voice.
Its pawprints burn the snow. Sprung

from measuring the first half of a life, it speaks
with gravity, the common weight that swings us.

It says, I've hidden, offered this side, that. And
sometimes too I'm buried in a blackness. Well,

here I am full upon you. Fall on your back. Or topple
me. What's wanted doesn't matter, nor even who

desires. Nor reason, much. Just fox.

## Le Cheval Blanc

> Beloved *is a word concealing*
> *four sharp points,*
> *four kinds of innocence,*
> *four winds of change.*
> —Chase Twichell, "Window in the Shape of a Diamond"

Our hotel room looks over snowy streets. We meet,
we climb unshovelled stairs, and each blind step's
a cavernous renewal. Inside, another flight, a narrow
winding through the prewar wood.

Having achieved Room 39, we rarely leave,
the pleas of cleaning staff a woeful stuttering
we wave, distractedly, away. The room is small,
the shower stall confessional; each vigorous lather

disencumbers the tortoiseshell comb of another
tooth. In the accumulated gloom our fingers
misremember truths, and history flickers,
qualifies, transmutes. Wrapped daily

in a blanket on the window seat I watch
you make the perilous descent
for coffee, and wonder at my limbs,
which have been hammered to an alloy

of apparently no weight, so that a gust
from the closing door unfurls me
like a scarf of smoke above the heads of stooped
pedestrians who watch their feet. Quasi

twilight: February streetlights belling the relentless
snow. Inside, *red smoke of blood,* a heavy
menstrual flow—which, oddly, like the twilight,
seems not mine, companionate—emblazons the white

sheets into the flag of a new country. We
assign this no more import than the fact
my luggage has gone missing, and all I have
is someone else's name, copied from an unclaimed

case that looked like mine. The night my clothes arrive
I dress; we brave the bitter wind for whisky, and later
for an ale that breathes raspberries, ghosts of summer,
in a tavern that will burn before the season's out.

That night doubt cracks us, and the open-
ended prospect of Room 39 accordions,
clamps shut. The heat-pipes rattle; snow muddles
all our tracks. There's no going back. Before

your hesitation I waver like a haunted leaf, of two
minds, holding on by one fierce wing. I shed
my clothes and cross a no man's land
to the window seat, where something of you

glimmers in the glassy dark. My spine
unlocks, and each familial link of logic
is catapulted through the pane. Reflected,
we exhale a contrail of assumptions, long

as ancestry, which snakes the drifted boulevard
and beads the lamps. I bow from the hip
to the jewelled street. I grip that threshold between
one story and the next, drive myself back into you.

# Farewell

I don't dream much of flying anymore. The technique
that hurled me over hydro wires into the whim
of a southwesterly or currents from a passing
goose's wing proves less effective with the years.

More often now I swim; on rare occasions
I push off from the ground: an intoxicating
endless step. The gesture's more controlled,
more willed, and deeply pleasing for that,

though I regret it's not as high. The last view
of my mother's yard the year she died
was flight-assisted. To launch my weight
a pole was needed, flexible and hollow,

roughly twice as long as I am tall. My breastbone
kissed its midpoint; I stretched arms along
its length, leaned into air, and leaped.
This pinion could be flapped to increase elevation;

I manoeuvered it to steer. In retrospect
my gradual ascent no doubt resembled
the slow takeoff of geese, who creak
their long farewell to lake and pasture.

I arrowed west, roof-high, along the lane behind
my mother's house, risking fascination
of a shirt-sleeved man at work who
dropped his rake and ran to pull me from the sky.

I laboured higher, circled back on that familiar lot,
its ill-kempt trees, starved lawn, its corners banked
with trash and blown silt. The yard was huge, the size
it must have been when I was young, surveyed

not in feet and inches but judged by
what it held, time twisting all the laws
of mass displaced. Below me, the tiny
swimming pool my father poured

and painted blue, mixing concrete in the shallow
wheelbarrow by hand. Where did he find
that shade of Hollywood azure that movie-
starred us in our plastic-flowered caps?

And there: the skating rink, a muddy hollow
he flooded with the garden hose late fall,
hardly larger than the grey back step
we huddled on to tie our skates. In those years

we were small; both parents had
a memory of what could please us.
Later: a pussy willow, and a curving escort
of bobbing white anemones along the path, which,

when the back fence grew from picket
to a six-foot plank, went nowhere prettily,
confounded by the mint green wall that kept
at bay the fruit thieves, the neighbour boys

who tossed crabapples at cars and broke
the trees. Nothing in the yard was new
since I had been there last. I circled it
for no more than a minute, then took

the usual route out of town, over
the cotoneaster hedge and through the corner lot,
up 16th, west to the coulees and the predictable
meander of the Old Man. And across.

# The Dream of the River

A coureur de bois, a man
                    *—the dreamer knows this*
*the way she knows awake she's female—*
                              I paddled,
with my male companion, laden with supplies
on a long journey up the river. We had little
for ourselves, a pot for cooking what we trapped,
the rice not ours: what I'd poured
into a bag was just enough, we hoped,
to save the lives of villagers upstream.
We had a bit of salmon kept as payment
for the guards. They would escort us through
a treacherous portage, and in exchange
we'd act the ritual they set. The ritual
would prove our mettle, purge our fault. And so
we dove into the river, swam underwater
through two joined corridors of pipe.

*The dreamer thinks the pipes not in themselves*
*significant, mere indicators of the time*
*and distance swum.*
                    We swam them both,
emerged in water limpid as a sunlit room.
The surface burned a long way up.
                              My friend,
suspended on the current, signed, his gesture
glimmeringly slow. That's when I knew.
The ritual decrees that air may be transferred;
it's adamant I may not help him swim.

*The dreamer apprehends this is a dream of*
*parting.*
          I exhaled a breath and watched him
gulp it. Not enough. His eyes met mine
still, lovingly.
                *The dreamer watches.*
The surface glittered overhead. Sick as I was
with love and sorrow, I knew my world. The voyage

wasn't done. Its tributaries, overhanging
brush, its rocks and rain.
*You're leaving something*
*out, the dreamer notes.*
I am. The wings.
Enormous, like a swan's, I saw them—
startled, then with recognition—beyond my shoulder
as we breast-stroked through the pipe.
Instead of dragging, waterlogged, as you might think,
they worked the current. An arrow flies; what I engaged
was muscular and hauled the water's mass.
I swam like a strong animal at home.
*And then?*
The wings guided me to my companion, pulsed
to hold me upright long enough to give him breath.
This felt very like a kiss, and was received so. Yes,
I admit that even in the dream I knew what moved me
to be wings. I felt both blessed and burdened—
the *called* that means responsible, that means you've
strength enough to carry out the task
you're given. Gifted, yes, but, ultimately,
disjoined from the beloved.
Judged by the gods or an afterworld.
Only partly there, and grasping
only a little of it.

## November, Early Morning

The cabin's honeyed walls
embrace: a curve
that can't believe I'm back, it's been so
long. The sun just beams.
It licks the stand of firs
to silhouettes, to their confirmed
best selves. Sunlight this deep in autumn
silvers, more like
the moon; it slinks, unfurling
over braes and dips and, molten,
seals the trunks. It pours
like speech or song over
the tongue of the furred earth.
A squirrel toys with gravity across
a gap. The straw of light
between this tree and that: so quick, so clean,
so transitory. Soon
late morning wind will sweep its hand through
this. But now each tree
is solidly its own, ink stroke
arrowed rock to sky. Some, thick,
have stuttered at the base, recovered
their trajectories. A few are flimsy
heartfelt leanings in thin light. All
knit midway in a shawl of common dark,
their singularity lost a while, and then
retrieved, but softened,
burred, a breath-end,
a staggered bearing
up.

## Root

*If you remove the number from objects, then everything
collapses.*
— Isidore of Seville, circa 600 A.D., plagiarizing Cassiodorus

As if to have these words said twice
would make them true. As if we numbered

loves. Are they not
one and one and one? As is

the present, to our touch: at
hand. What gathers

and disperses takes us
with it, pollinates: articulate

displacement. Here's
to the unnumbered, the spilled

vessel, cracked and patched
and filled again, wave upon

particular. There is a tree
unremarked at any other season,

which, in the mountains during June, floods
its common saw-toothed leaves

with cornucopias of milky bloom.
Good natured. If I knew its name .

it wouldn't engage me so. I wouldn't note
the texture of its bark, the way

its leaves respond to light, its graceful
sprawl of limbs and mild canopy.

The square root of anything
is wondrous nonsense, leads us

only where we might have thought to go.
Who'd think to count the petals

shivered loose by morning wind
and forecast thunder? I change my route

to pass their shimmer, and today
pursue the luminous

slur of flakes down to the river. Without
saying, ah me,

and you, of course, it goes. The petals leave
their family tree, soft barnacles unbuttoned.

Imagine a gale, imagine wind
whipped blonde, imagine muslin, magnified

to sheer distraction. Why not,
*if you remove the number,*

*everything assumes*
*an implication, a progression,*

and augers, ouroboros, into
more? What Isidore argues

is a world view, based on fear,
that's minimized, aligned, reduced

to tool. It terminates. It sutures. *Our days*
*are numbered.* No, they're not, unless we

count them. Ye gods and little fishes, who
is he trying to fool?

## Green Light

Did people walk more slowly? Past centuries, I mean.
Who might have studied this? I wonder, stepping
past only the second deer I've seen, a doe, lying at rest
a few feet from the path. What permission
might we need? For such completeness to our days,
task-free. She watches me but doesn't stir,
not when I'm going or coming back, so what I carry
is no matter, though between us. How
does she judge me, then? Speed of my gait,
direction of my gaze? Her ears flick when I speak,
but this results in nothing I can read. Beyond us,

snowlit mountains, tawny river flats between.
And, winding the bridge into the streets
named for the banished mammals, the flit
of sun on painted steel. Tiny, we humans,
alarming in our brute persistence. One
could despair, or die of it. Or let ourselves
a place in the exquisite hive, accept
the slur of the unformed, shed our brittle
exo-worldly-skeletons. We could be,
only more so. We could meet the world.

# Notes

"Dial": According to Lawrence Wright in *Clockwork Man,* "A 24-hour mechanical clock, laid face upwards, is a model of the revolving earth (represented by the index or hour-hand) in its positions relative to the sun or stars (represented by the hour-marks)."

"46 B.C.": To bring the Roman calendar back into alignment with the vernal equinox, in 46 B.C. Julius Caesar ordered, among other changes, the insertion of two extra intercalary months between November and December. 46 B.C. was popularly known as the Year of Confusion.

"The Great Astronomical Clock...": Boccaccio, writing of the speed with which the plague struck, said its victims often "ate lunch with their friends and dinner with their ancestors in paradise."

"Residual": An eagle bone dating from 11,000 B.C., found in the Dordogne Valley, bears markings which indicate its use as an early lunar calendar.

"Another Rhapsody": The quoted phrase in stanza 4 is from part 2 of Mary Oliver's "Work" in *The Leaf and the Cloud.* The poem is for Sina.

"Savasana": *Savasana* is Sanskrit for the Corpse Pose in yoga practice.

"*Tuck Everlasting*": *Tuck Everlasting* is the title of Natalie Babbitt's classic children's novel (Farrar, Straus and Giroux, 1975).

"*Le Cheval Blanc*" is in part a response to Chase Twichell's poem "Window in the Shape of a Diamond" in *Perdido.* The quoted phrase in stanza 6 is from "Lapses of Turquoise Sea" in the same collection.

## Acknowledgements

I'm grateful to the Canada Council for its support during the writing of these poems, and to those who operate the Leighton Studio program at the Banff Centre, where most of the poems were written.

"Dial" and "Pocketwatch" were awarded Silver for Poetry at the National Magazine Awards in 2004. I'm much obliged to the editors of *PRISM international*, in which the poems first appeared, and to those at *Arc*, who first published "Another Rhapsody."

Thanks to all the folks at Brick for their care and attention, especially Clare Goulet and Don McKay.

My thanks and love to Mitch—for time together and time apart.

*M*arlene Cookshaw was born and raised in southern Alberta and now lives on Pender Island, B.C. *Lunar Drift* is her fifth book of poetry, and the fourth to be published by Brick Books. *Shameless* (2002), was shortlisted for the Dorothy Livesay Poetry Prize and the Pat Lowther Award. Cookshaw has received the Robinson Jeffers Tor House Prize for Poetry and the Ralph Gustafson Poetry Prize. She has served on juries for various writing awards, and had a long association with *The Malahat Review*, most recently as editor. Her other Brick books are *Double Somersaults, Shameless,* and *The Whole Elephant.*